Country Style Kitchens

An Inspiring Design Guide

Country Style Kitchens

Tina Skinner

An Inspiring Design Guide

Acknowledgements

To Melissa Cardona for getting this project underway; best of luck in future endeavors. To Nathaniel Wolfgang-Price, a cheerful helper ever ready to carry the ball. Most importantly, to the designers represented in this book, credited and anonymous, who helped to fashion these inspiring rooms.

Cover images courtesy of Hearthstone Homes, The Hardwood Council, and Zook Custom Kitchens . Back cover image courtesy of Wood-Mode Incorporated.

Copyright © 2006 by Schiffer Publishing, Ltd.
Library of Congress Control Number: 2006927234

Designed by John P. Cheek
Cover design by Bruce Waters
Type set in Cooper Lt BT/Humanist 521 BT

ISBN: 0-7643-2490-X
Printed in China

Published by Schiffer Publishing Ltd.
4880 Lower Valley Road
Atglen, PA 19310
Phone: (610) 593-1777; Fax: (610) 593-2002
E-mail: Info@schifferbooks.com

For the largest selection of fine reference books on this and related subjects, please visit our web site at
www.schifferbooks.com
We are always looking for people to write books on new and related subjects. If you have an idea for a book please contact us at the above address.

This book may be purchased from the publisher.
Include $3.95 for shipping.
Please try your bookstore first.
You may write for a free catalog.

In Europe, Schiffer books are distributed by
Bushwood Books
6 Marksbury Ave.
Kew Gardens
Surrey TW9 4JF England
Phone: 44 (0) 20 8392-8585; Fax: 44 (0) 20 8392-9876
E-mail: info@bushwoodbooks.co.uk
Website: www.bushwoodbooks.co.uk
Free postage in the U.K., Europe; air mail at cost.

Contents

The Elements of Country

Trend analysts are talking about the latest wave of "suburban blight" as people flee the suburbs for even further reaches. The quest, it seems, is for a sense of belonging to the land. Homes on large tracts of acreage are the highly-sought "gentlemen's farms." Sometimes these are the original farmhouses, refurbished and expanded to meet today's expectations of luxury living. Other times they are new construction built to intimate earlier times. Today's popular houses often incorporate the look of multiple rooflines, like those created for Victorians at the last turn of a century. Various ells and extensions receive differing facings – part stone, part clapboard, part brick – to give a sense of decades of family growth and prosperity. Inside, the same multi-generation character is desired, imbuing a home with the feeling that the family has revolved around this site for centuries.

Country style, once defined as white geese with blue bows around their necks, is much more sophisticated today. Farmhouse style and the charms of hand-crafted country treasures are evoked more subtly for today's homeowners, the looks often enhanced with aesthetics imported by earlier generation, imbued old world charm from the farmhouses of Provance, Tuscany, or the gentle English countryside.

This book visits some of the European influences on country style, as well as a smattering of Americana. The focus, however, is on the colors, the textures, and the elements that evoke a farmhouse setting, while providing contemporary comfort and convenience to modern households. Some of the elements that make for country style are defined an illustrated in the first half of the book. These same elements crop up time and again in the many beautiful kitchens profiled in the second half.

The goal, when all is said and done, and every last page and beautiful kitchen is examined, is to inspire homeowners and designers to add the warmth and personality that make a kitchen their own, and a welcome haven to friend and family.

The Architecture

In the not-so long-ago times, a kitchen was a place where the industry of cooking took place. The dining, the family gathering, and most certainly the entertaining, was conducted in more formal settings. The kitchen received little attention as to decoration, and during hot summer months might even be relocated to a removed structure separate from the people.

So what one might find in the kitchen of yore would be the ruder elements of the architecture – the raw wood, brick, and stone of the actual structure, the hearth where fires were tended for the sole purpose of preparing food, and in the poorest of hovels, a modest table where a small family might gather to share a hard-earned meal.

Today those same elements lend grace and value to a very different kitchen atmosphere. Wood, brick, and stone – once integral to the actual structure – are now added as decorative elements. Arched hoods and surrounds mimic the old wood hearth in kitchens, albeit overlooking vast, eight-range gas burners today. And the thoughtful home designer, with space to spare, might incorporate an actual fireplace in the kitchen environment, to add the nostalgic flicker of flame to the contemporary cooking center.

One feels they've entered a kitchen furnished with antiques carefully treasured over generations. In fact, the homeowner discovered the massive armoire in the corner during a trip abroad. The remainder of the "antiques" are newly created by Rutt Studio of Mainland/Wayne, PA. The 48-inch range is housed in a brick enclosure lined with glazed European tiles. Designers Julie Stoner, CKD, ASID, and Mari Dolby Interiors of Berwyn, PA *Courtesy of National Kitchen and Bath Association*

Wood, Brick, and Stone

As these and other images throughout the book illustrate, the beauty of natural materials is part and parcel of the "country feel" for a kitchen. Heavier elements like stone and brick are often incorporated to simulate "historic" walls. Wooden beams, whether part of the actual roof support or simply an aesthetic embellishment, are enviable elements in a kitchen, and country cabinetry styles are invariably in keeping with early cabinetmaker's creations dating back over 100 years.

David Van Scott Photography

Wood, brick, and stone stand side-by-side at the modern cook's hearth, evocative of kitchens past, while imbued with today's most modern cooking technology. (For more images of this kitchen, see Page 107.) *Courtesy of Zook Custom Kitchens*

Opposite page:
Blue cabinetry adds counterpoint to a room rich with wooden architecture – log walls and exposed ceiling beams. *Courtesy of Hearthstone Homes*

Rich Frutchey & Associates Photography

Log home construction follows the tradition of the earliest homes built in the United States. Today, such construction is a natural for anyone hoping to establish a home that will hold its value and appeal for generations to come. A natural finish on the cabinetry, wide-plank pine floors, and a stone hearth imbue this home with priceless natural elements. *Courtesy of Hearthstone Homes*

Exposed beams reveal the secret behind a soaring cathedral ceiling, in a kitchen where sophistication is unparalleled, but charm is maintained. Ironwork in the light fixtures and semi-formal cabinetry evoke a sense of the country estate. *Courtesy of Wood-Mode Incorporated*

Beadboard paneling adds country charm to an eating area in an informal kitchen. Blue and white china further the sense of delight. *Courtesy of Glidden paints*

A central island in brick creates a solid centerpiece for this generous kitchen, adding a sense of permanence to the space. *Courtesy of Canyon Creek Cabinet Company*

Sunny yellow on a brick wall adds contemporary flair to a space that seems to bridge two generations. *Courtesy of Glidden paints*

Wallpaper simulates brick, creating a desired illusion and negating the need for floor reinforcement required for brick facing! *Courtesy of Village, F. Schumacher & Co.*

The Hearth

An arched opening, underlined with brick facing on the back wall, creates an illusion of the a hearth, and a sense of history.
Courtesy of Mouser Custom Cabinetry

Above:
A brick "hearth" is the centerpiece for this massive kitchen, the lower and upper hearths echoing the design of a wood-burning oven. The green crown and grey brick hark back to an Italian heritage. *Courtesy of Wellborn Cabinet, Inc.*

Top right:
Once a housewife might have needed this hearth to prepare her stew. Today a woodstove insert creates a compelling warmth for the family gathered here to dine. *Courtesy of Barbara Herr Kitchens*

Bottom right:
A sturdy brick surround houses the cook center, and provides quick access to the cook's tools and seasonings. (For more images of this kitchen, see Page 120-121.) *Courtesy of Jon Jahr & Associates*

An arched opening in the cabinetry surround carries on tradition, with the added convenience of a very contemporary double oven and range.
Courtesy of Barbara Herr Kitchens

A commercial-quality range nestles beneath an arched wood panel supported by corbels, making it the focal point of an expansive kitchen area. *Courtesy of National Kitchen and Bath Association*

A wood surround and "mantel" form a hearthspace for a cook's fantasy. As in the hearth cooksites of yesteryear, a tool rack provides handy storage for spoons, ladles, pots and the other accouterments of cusine. *Courtesy of Bis Bis Imports, Boston*

It's only for effect, but an arched tile inset over the stove harks back to the hearth, creating a pretty focal point. *Courtesy of Mouser Custom Cabinetry*

Eat-In Kitchens

Today's homes often allot a substantial portion of the square footage to a kitchen area, which is often part of, or open to, the main living areas of the home. While a major trend in kitchen design has been to incorporate barstool seating at a central island, those going for a more traditional feel in their kitchens prefer an actual table and chairs within the work area, where family members can gather.

Elizabeth Shapiro Murphy, ASID

In the traditional American home, families took their daily meals in the kitchen, and moved to a formal dining room when company came calling. Besides serving as the central dining space, a kitchen table also enhanced workspace in a room that was often limited in size.
Courtesy of Elizabeth Shapiro Murphy Interior Design

A space-saving seating arrangement, benches help pack in the bodies. In this case, a padded window seat is also a favorite hangout between meals, and a great strategy for a cook who wants to lure company into her midst. Courtesy of Kitchens Concepts & Roomspaces, Inc.

Left:
Wicker adds texture to this country kitchen, and comfort to those seated at a pretty round table. *Courtesy of Waverly, F. Schumacher & Co.*

Right:
Caning makes formal wooden chairs more farm-friendly for casual kitchen dining, surrounded by warm colors and a foliage motif. *Courtesy of Waverly, F. Schumacher & Co.*

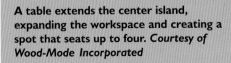

A table extends the center island, expanding the workspace and creating a spot that seats up to four. *Courtesy of Wood-Mode Incorporated*

John Meixner Photography

Above & left:
A colorful table backs up to bench seating. At left, A special dog bed and enhanced dining area has been provided for a pampered pet. (For more images of this kitchen, see page 86-88.) *Courtesy of Mannarino Designs, Inc.*

Right:
A simple pine hutch, a display of enamel dinnerware, basketry, and a pretty floral border add up to down-home charm. *Courtesy of Village, F. Schumacher & Co.*

Furnishings

The Hutch

In many cases, the effect of country and continuity is created using mismatched elements. New and old "antique" pieces are paired, formal and informal and put together in purposeful contradiction, and contemporary appliances sit in juxtaposition to primitive fixtures. The desired effect is an overall sense that a kitchen space has organically evolved through generations.

Another new built-in takes on the patina of age with a display of treasured antiques. *Courtesy of Mouser Custom Cabinetry*

Most historic homes lay claim to built-in corner cabinetry, much of which has been plundered for a rich antique resale market. Today we're creating such treasure for future generations in our kitchens. *Courtesy of Kountry Kraft, Inc.*

Beadboard fronts and pharmacist drawers draw on tradition, and an antique finish adds the possibility that this new cabinetry unit could be antique. *Courtesy of StarMark Cabinetry*

A birch "hutch" with copper stain cleverly houses a wet bar complete with a concealed mini fridge. *Designed by Christopher Jacobs, CKD; Courtesy of Keener Kitchen Manufacturing Co.*

A custom-painted finish makes this look like a long-loved family treasure. *Designed by Christopher Jacobs, CKD; Courtesy of Keener Kitchen Manufacturing*

Today's hutch performs functions our ancestors never imagined, here housing the indispensable microwave oven. *Courtesy of Kountry Kraft, Inc.*

Legs on custom cabinetry add the illusion that this is a piece of heirloom furniture. Built-in lighting adds to the efficiency and appeal. *Courtesy of Crystal Cabinet Works*

A pretty hutch in two tones creates an opportunity for both storage and display. *Courtesy of Merillat*

An old-fashioned-looking hutch needn't be. Here a mini-fridge has been carefully fitted into the side of a custom-made hutch. The wood tones work to add character to a contemporary kitchen setting. (For another view of this kitchen, see Page 82) *Courtesy of K T Highland, Inc.*

Tom Young Photography

Independent Islands

Islands have become virtual must-haves in today's spacious kitchens. They make a large room feel more intimate, and they add workspace as well as gathering stations for family and friends. For the country look, these island units often take the form of oversized kitchen tables, or giant butcher blocks. Their seeming independence lends them the air of heirloom, and the room the resulting sense of antiquity.

At counter height, a central table was crafted to look one hundred years old, with a finish sturdy enough to withstand a century of hard use. *Courtesy of Signature Custom Cabinetry, Inc.; Design Firm: Saw Horse Designs - Millburn, NJ*

A central butcher-block island features a broad work surface, and a big shelf perfect for storing oversize serving dishes and cookware. *Courtesy of Bruce Hardwood Floors from Armstrong*

A warm green finish adds antique patina to a massive butcher-block island unit. *Courtesy of Wellborn Cabinet, Inc.*

An antique dresser was converted with a nice wood counter and now serves as a central island in a charming country kitchen. *Courtesy of Village, F. Schumacher & Co.*

An open island unit crowns a wood floor with a pretty parquetry finish. *Courtesy of Glidden paints*

Open Shelves

The informal effect of shelves left open to view is perfect for the country kitchen, evocative of times when kitchen elements were for effect, not affect. Still, the opportunity to embellish them with pretty displays is irresistible, and even everyday dinnerware is afforded the opportunity to become part of the décor.

A simple hutch, a great working sink area, and a bracketed shelf are indicative of the furnishings our great grandparents probably enjoyed. Today, painted a pretty powder blue, and presented just so, they're highly desirable elements in a cook's kitchen. *Courtesy of Bis Bis Imports, Boston*

A simple, straightforward corner shelving unit becomes a note of nostalgia in a sentimental country kitchen. *Courtesy of Village, F. Schumacher & Co.*

Open shelving is an efficient way to store oversize pieces while simultaneously showing them off.
Courtesy of Glidden paints

Two tiers of shelving overhang an eating island, adding storage to a space where a landscape of open, sunny walls has been carefully preserved. *Courtesy of Village, F. Schumacher & Co.*

A wall of cabinetry combines efficient locker-like storage serving sentry to open shelving above a sink and food prep area. *Courtesy of Bis Bis Imports, Boston*

A simple shelving unit on the dining wall, and a hutch with more open storage, underline a connection with simpler times. *Courtesy of Village, F. Schumacher & Co.*

Her tools at the ready, a cook keeps a coat rack on hand for the tools of her trade. *Courtesy of Village, F. Schumacher & Co.*

Two cabinetry units recall hutch construction, while expanding the capacity greatly. Together they create an informal mix of windows, beadboard doors, and open shelves. *Courtesy of Merillat*

Window cabinetry and open shelves create attractive, informal storage space for a kitchen and pantry area. *Courtesy of Village, F. Schumacher & Co.*

The Farmer's Sink

If one element alone were to define the sense of country kitchen today, it's the farmer's sink. A big, rectangular basin, today's designers often seek out the more primitive materials of past sink manufacture – soapstone, concrete, and other stones being among the current favorites.

The deep skirt of a farmer's sink typifies today's perception of a country kitchen. It also provides the homeowner with a practical workspace for wet jobs. Paired with a raised faucet, like this one, it also makes filling and washing deep pots a simpler task.
Courtesy of Plain & Fancy Custom Cabinetry

Reminiscent of drysinks of yesteryear, this cabinetry unit is capped by a pretty sink and countertop cleverly designed to contain runoff while looking wonderful. *Courtesy of Downsview Kitchens*

In the old world, plate racks topped sinks, allowing just-washed dishes to drip dry. A unique bonnet top amoire houses two refrigerators. *Designed by Cindy Myers, CKD; Courtesy of Keener Kitchen Manufacturing Company*

45

A deep farmer's sink and fully integrated dishwasher are the centerpieces of a pretty custom unit that looks timeless in its design. *Courtesy of Kitchen Concepts & Roomscapes, Inc.*

Antique glass, peckie cypress cabinetry, and a country-style sink blend with granite countertops in this Texas ranch. *Courtesy of JAY Interiors, Inc.*

White and green pair for a clean, fresh feeling kitchen. The farmer's sink and simple display create simple country appeal. *Courtesy of Village, F. Schumacher & Co.*

Stainless steel is actually a return to tradition, and the appeal continues. *Courtesy of Signature Custom Cabinetry, Inc.;* Design Firm: Saw Horse Designs - Millburn, NJ

A copper sink creates a warm centerpiece in this kitchen. *Courtesy of Stone Forest*

Another example of a stainless steel farmer's sink, offering an abundance of dish-stacking space. *Courtesy of Signature Custom Cabinetry, Inc.;* Design Firm: Lobkovich Kitchen Designs - Vienna, VA

Close-up images illustrate textures available in stone and metal for today's sink shopper. *Courtesy of Stone Forest*

A hand-painted farmer's sink in enamel harks back to the European ancestry of our farm heritage. *Courtesy of Mannarino Designs, Inc.*

The Feel

The big-ticket items like furnishings, cabinetry, and appliances chosen, the real weight of country-style results after the accouterments are added. Playful and generous applications of color are integral to most people's sense of what constitutes country. Primitive, regional, or sentimental antiques may play a big part in the presentation. Folk art helps add aura, and so do motifs involving nature and animals. Texture, too, is an important aspect of what creates a country feeling, from pretty textiles to natural wood grains and hand-forged iron. Beyond that, it's just how the space is lived in — the pots and pans hanging ready for fixing food, herbs drying fresh from the kitchen garden, and baskets ready to load up for picnics and country socials. After all, the first step toward living the country life, is preparing for it!

Use of Color

Blue is far and away the favorite among those who prefer a country kitchen, but other primary colors are gaining. Barn red is a front runner, and a rich green is finding preference. More contemporary country designs are often brightened with mood enhancing yellows. Whatever your preference, the following images are sure to send you running for sample paint strips.

Blue does the primary job of turning this kitchen "country." The setting is modern, with raised ceiling and big picture windows. The blue, combined with a traditional family table, create an informal farmhouse feel for a suburban home. *Courtesy of The Kitchen Guild*

A "Garden Room" blue
lends an aura of antiq-
uity to this space.
*Courtesy of Barbara Herr
Kitchens*

Blue-grey finish adds an
historic authenticity to a
kitchen crafted of fine
hardwoods. *Courtesy of the
Hardwood Council*

Blue walls provide compliment to wood cabinetry, a classic combination.
Courtesy of KraftMaid Cabinetry

Left & Far left:
Multi-tones of blue and white, and an antique finish add texture and patina to this blue kitchen. *Courtesy of Glidden paints*

A bright blue makes it spring forever in a kitchen overflowing with happy. *Courtesy of Downsview Kitchens*

A painted floor provides a platform for sky blues in this cheerful setting. *Courtesy of Glidden paints*

One of the latest trends in kitchen design is to combine laundry facilities with the cook center. One more way that mom can multi-task! Here her work station is done in the colors of the flag for the all-American lifestyle. *Courtesy of KraftMaid Cabinetry*

A mix of primary colors ads contemporary country flair to a kitchen. The country hutch, painted barn red, is a focal point in the sunny space. *Courtesy of Glidden paints*

A mix of blue and yellow, with a smattering of wood and red, add a sense of the southwest in this country-style kitchen. Tile backsplashes play with a seemingly random repeat of diamond motifs. *Courtesy of Quality Custom Cabinetry*

Barn red plays backup to a subtle symphony of country motifs, from hearts hanging on the wall, to primitive crocks displayed in glass-front cabinets. *Courtesy of Gehman Custom Remodeling*

State-of-the-art stainless steel appliances cozy into brick-red cabinetry, which warms their effect in this spacious kitchen. *Courtesy of Susan Cohen Associates, Inc.*

A convenient stand trundles to wher-ever it's needed. Two-tones of green provide a landscape for bright yellow and red accents throughout this kitchen. *Courtesy of Glidden paints*

Black countertop and backsplash provide counterpoint to a warm shade of green and light colored ceilings, at home in the rolling hills of the countryside. *Courtesy of Kitchen Concepts & Roomscapes, Inc.*

John Ferrarone Photography

A bluish-green cast adds antiquity to built-in cabinetry. *Courtesy of Bruce Hardwood Floors from Armstrong*

Grey green cabinetry and nostalgic plaid wallpaper create the kitchen of yesteryear. *Courtesy of Village, F. Schumacher & Co.*

Faded black cabinetry, with a mat sheet, harkens back to the moldings and panelings of past decades.
Courtesy of Hearthstone Homes

Antique finishes on the furnishings and reproduction appliances are some of the ways in which a sense of timelessness can be introduced to a kitchen. *Courtesy of Elmira Stove Works*

Farm Animals and Other Motifs

It sounds so corny. We thought we'd gotten away from the geese with bowties. However, a colorful rooster has timeless appeal, and a spotted cow still carries the rural message home. A few barnyard reminders establish a sense of place, and connectedness, in the kitchen. Throughout the book you'll see that many designers have inserted a subtle barnyard icon. Even more subtle, floral motifs provide an element of nature, and nostalgia. After all, grandma loved to fill her kitchen with flowers. We've not grown too sophisticated to appreciate the appeal of blooms, have we?

Grey Crawford Photography

There she is, a mother hen and her chicks parading in front of the window. Closer to home, a "chicken wire" basket serves eggs. These are subtle barnyard icons in a room dominated by a stunning wood floor. *Courtesy of Henry Johnstone & Co.*

John Ferrarone Photography

John Herr Photography

A kitchen perfectly crafted for today's active lifestyle offers clues to a yearning for farm-connectedness – fowl art plays a staring role above the range, and the combination of three wood species gives a warm welcome. *Courtesy of Kitchen Concepts & Roomscapes, Inc.*

A rooster and a cow claim real estate in this handsome kitchen, imbued with historic nostalgia. *Courtesy of Barbara Herr Kitchens*

Farmyard fowl have long inspired artists, and their beauty been proudly displayed. *Courtesy of Village, F. Schumacher & Co.*

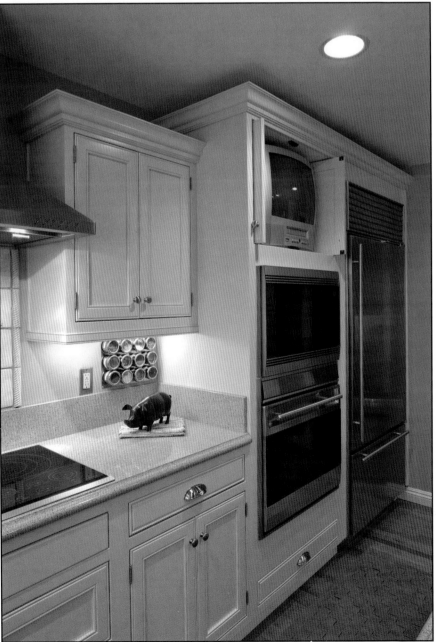

A bronze pig holds a place in a compact kitchen, adding a note of personality to a small kitchen with little space to spare. *Courtesy of Canyon Creek Cabinet Company*

Pig trivets add a touch of whimsey to a collection of antique molds and kitchen tools.
A gas lamp, and an old-fashioned faucet are part of the rich detailing that provide a
sense of history for this kitchen. *Courtesy of Plain & Fancy Custom Cabinetry*

A sheepish character occupies counterspace, overlooked by the swine set carefully housed behind chicken wire. (For more images of this kitchen, see Page 71.) *Courtesy of Montana Avenue Interiors*

Okay, so we still have geese, but these are ever-so elegant within their dining room setting. *Courtesy of Montana Avenue Interiors*

Home Sweet Home

An apple tree and wallpaper borders are an unabashed display of cheerful country gaiety. *Courtesy of Village, F. Schumacher & Co.*

Texture and Textiles

The loving details are what warm a country kitchen is all about. Handpainted pottery and furnishings, cheerful curtains, table runners, and napkins, and pretty accents like potholders and throw rugs. When it comes to country, it's hard to overdo. Minimalism is a hard act to pull off if you want to feel "farmhouse." As you admire images throughout the book, you will notice that it is the details, such as the textiles, that tend to draw you in.

Pretty floral curtains coordinate the red and cream tones of a kitchen, and a custom island resembling a farm table completes the setting. *Courtesy of Kitchen Concepts & Roomspaces, Inc.*

A roman shade and rustic tile add texture to this kitchen setting. *Courtesy of Thomas Bartlett Interiors*

Filmy curtains accent enviable picture windows, while a heart-shaped braided rug adds that nostalgic country touch below. *Courtesy of Mouser Custom Cabinetry*

A profusion of flowers on the wall, draped chairs, and a floor-to-ceiling drape combine for feminine allure. *Courtesy of Waverly, F. Schumacher & Co.*

Copper Pots, Baskets, and Hanging Herbs

When we hang our pots on display, or hang herbs to dry, we surround ourselves with icons that indicate place. After all, a kitchen is a place of industry, where food is produced for both daily and future consumption. The historic connection between kitchen and garden was intimate. The proximity of food to frying pan imperative. Today these elements may be simply decorative, or they may help stimulate a return to what we build kitchens for – the artistry and industry of food production.

Pretty tile adorns the walls, just as it surrounded hearths in olden days. The sophististry of blue and white glaze serves perfect foil to a rustic work table and a collection of oft-used copper cookware. *Courtesy of Susan Cohen Associates, Inc.*

Dedicated to cooking, this kitchen is endowed with an Aga cooker. Pots and pans hang at the ready above. *Courtesy of Kathryn Scott Design Studios, Ltd.*

A sense of Nordic pioneerism is conveyed in a kitchen, with the rudiments of food preparation and storage space along walls free of enclosed cabinetry. *Courtesy of Wood-Mode Incorporated*

Hanging garlic, basketry, and fresh flowers add rural accessories to a wonderful, modern kitchen. *Courtesy of Kountry Kraft, Inc.*

Copper pots take center stage over bar seating that overlooks the cook's work area. *Courtesy of Thomas Bartlett Interiors*

A hanging pot rack was once standard equipment for cookcenters. Today they serve as embellishment.
Courtesy of Merillat

Left:
Steel pots likewise lend themselves to display, adding sparkle
and diffusing canister lights above. Here they are suspended
from an antique wooden ladder. *Courtesy of K T Highland, Inc.*

A Tour of Terrific Country Kitchens

Here is a wonderful kitchen, replete with the elements that help to define country style: mix-and-match cabinetry and furnishings, a hearth, and the accouterments and motifs that define setting. *Courtesy of Kountry Kraft, Inc.*

The primary colors make this kitchen sing with country flair, inspired by the French countryside, but personalized to fit the owner's sense of fun. Roosters parade throughout, amidst flowers and fruit. *Courtesy of Mannarino Designs*

John Meixner Photography

Francois   Jacques   Marcel

Personalized touches include a wine center in the pantry area, a desk area, and a special bed for a beloved pet under the kitchen table. *Courtesy of Mannarino Designs*

A parquet floor was created with two tones of stain on a wide-plank foor. The charming effect serves as pretty underline to a kitchen with cabinetry done in two tones, setting the island apart. *Courtesy of KraftMaid Cabinetry*

A painted pine-plank floor adds zest to a beautiful, but compact, kitchen. *Courtesy of Glidden Paints*

Tile adds contrast to a handsome kitchen, with two-tone cabinetry styled in an Arts-and-Crafts period sensibility straight out of the 1920s. *Courtesy of Kountry Kraft, Inc.*

Left:
Wide-plank flooring with an antique finish creates a sense of antiquity for this room. The sensibility was sustained with new cabinetry featuring bead-board panels for rustic flair. *Courtesy of KraftMaid Cabinetry*

Below:
Reclaimed barn doors are a personal touch in a kitchen packed with personalized charm. Mixed finishes on the cabinetry, and a reproduction stove are among the amenities that create a country atmosphere within a new home setting. *Courtesy of Timberpeg®*

91

An oak floor with a clear finish underlines a contemporary kitchen with decorative elements that hark back to simpler times, like the mantle-like hood over the cook range, and carved legs that lend a sense of heirloom furniture to the island. *Courtesy of Crystal Cabinet Works*

Rustic wood cabinetry, wide-plank flooring, and exposed ceiling beams create a nostalgic environment for the handcrafted domestic environments of yesteryear.
Courtesy of KraftMaid Cabinetry

A simple woven rug underlies the simplicity of a kitchen eating area furnished with casual furniture and a wood hutch, and lovingly lavished with floral wallpaper. *Courtesy of Village, F. Schumacher & Co.*

A huge hearth is in scale with this expansive country kitchen. Here, the family enjoys a dining table under the same coffered ceiling as the cook area, as well as the option of seating along the lengthy island bar area. *Courtesy of Wood-Mode Incorporated*

Placing wood flooring at an angle actually helps expand the sense of space in a limited kitchen. Beaded paneling in a footed island and a butcher-block counter lend a country twist to this clean-styled kitchen. *Courtesy of Ulrich, Inc.*

John Schwartz Photography

A warm and comforting, timeless mix was created by surrounding a few, simple, antique furnishings with textiles, wallpaper, and wood paneling. *Courtesy of Waverly, F. Schumacher & Co.*

Varying cabinet heights, colors, and countertop heights helps to break up the landscape in this massive, open kitchen area. *Courtesy of Merillat*

Rich cherry-toned cabinetry and a matching range hood add warmth to this open kitchen. A central island in white bead-board is the centerpiece within this setting. *Courtesy of Mouser Custom Cabinetry*

All the elements of antiquity exist or were created for this alluring space. Within the architectural riches of stone wall, antique plank flooring, and exposed wood ceiling, a mix of cabinetry has been created. Rustic cherry and painted units were paired with antiqued cabinetry, all capped with user-friendly wood countertop. Varying countertop heights add to the sense that this kitchen evolved organically through multiple generations. *Courtesy of Zook Custom Kitchens*

David Van Scott Photography

A sense of nature is conveyed throughout a large kitchen replete with woodwork, from floor to ceiling, culminating in a massive stone hearth on the far wall. *Courtesy of Wood-Mode Incorporated*

A farmers sink and an antique grey patina add a sense of establishment to a the new kitchen created for a 100-year-old farmhouse. A window seat snugged up to the stretch of view-filled window, is a magnet for family members. *Courtesy of Nancy Van Natta Associates*

Vince Valdez. Photographer

A timber frame supports the open floorplan of a kitchen, dining, and living room. Though timber framing was used by the earliest pioneers to put up homes in the United States, the open floor plan is a newly popular concept in family living. *Courtesy of Hearthstone Homes*

Two-tones of cabinetry create an impression of an antique hutch nestled into the corner of this kitchen. A natural finish was used on the pine paneled ceiling, floor, and even the panels concealing a modern refrigerator. *Courtesy of Canyon Creek Cabinetry Company*

A hearth, surrounded in stone and backed in herring-bone-pattern brick, serves as the central focal point in a kitchen evocative of days past. Substantial wooden beams crisscross the ceiling, and wide planks underline the space. *Courtesy of Zook Custom Kitchens*

David Van Scott Photography

Cream-colored finish on the cabinetry and walls brightens the room, accented by appetizing fruit and foliage motifs. *Designed by Stephen T. Keener, CMKBD, President of Keener Kitchen Manufacturing Company*

Antiqued blue and white create an appealing environment, adding patina to the shiny copper cookware and stainless steel appliances. *Courtesy of Thermador*

Nestled under the slope of a cathedral celing, a warm, wood-toned kitchen was given furniture-like detailing and a tiled "hearth" over the range. *Courtesy of Mouser Custom Cabinetry*

Fresh mint and sky blue brighten this space, keeping it fresh and inviting. Country elements like open shelving and a farmer's sink that coordinates with the clean white countertops were included to add to the comfort level. *Courtesy of Glidden paints*

Bench seating expands the capacity of an informal kitchen table. Roosters and a farmer's sink establish the homeowners' sentiments. "Wormy" English white oak lend both durability and visual strength to the room, yet still provide the patina of aged wood specified by the clients. *Courtesy of Ulrich, Inc.*

"Farmer's Market" over the sink proclaims a cook's fancy for the freshest ingredients in her gourmet kitchen. *Courtesy of KraftMaid Cabinetry*

Mixed textures and colors – blue and yellow plaid, beadboard cabinetry, and a fresh-fruit motif – combine for country charm. *Courtesy of Waverly, F. Schumacher & Co.*

Mixed elements in the cabinetry and furnishings establish a sense of history. Embellishments include hand-crafted items for a rustic effect. *Courtesy of Charlotte Comers Interiors, Inc.*

A hearth area surrounds the cook center, and open shelving announces the culinary treasures of this home. Note the unique, and handy, built-in towel rack at the ready by the farmer's sink. *Courtesy of Signature Custom Cabinetry, Inc.; Design Firm: Bailey Avenue Kitchens - Ridgefield, CT*

A pretty red pantry was imbued with charm, from the toile swag curtain to the latticework wallpaper. The space strikes a wonderful balance between the need for storage and the desire for display. *Courtesy of Interior Decisions, MC.*

White updates the look of a beamed space, while a display of basketry keeps the kitchen grounded in tradition. *Courtesy of Montana Avenue Interiors*

Various angles explore a kitchen overlooked, seemingly, by a fireplace – the lit brick cook center that forms the "hearth" of this expansive kitchen nestled beneath the soaring beams of the timber-frame house. A great butcher-block island serves as the central work area, with storage underneath and seating on three sides. *Courtesy of Jon Jahr & Associates*

Just a few red gingham accents repeated throughout this kitchen are enough to evoke nostalgia for country picnics and church socials. *Courtesy of StarMark Cabinetry*

A rug completes the look of this room, tying together the colors of walls, accessories, and the antique cream finish. "Driving the design aesthetic was the notion that the kitchen should resemble a room that had taken shape over a long period of time," said designers Alan Asarnow and Holly Rickert. This was accomplished by specifying cabinets to be partially unfitted, and made from different styles, species, and finishes. *Courtesy of Ulrich, Inc.*

Though our ancestors may not have bellied up to bars in their kitchens, today's furniture designers have adapted the traditional Windsor chair to the popular new pastime. This kitchen combines elements evocative of yesterday's antiques, though in a purely modern setting. The one exception is the warmth of a real fire in the fireplace, a sentimental touch within a centrally heated environment. *Courtesy of Barbara Herr Kitchens*

John Herr Photography

A warm wood finish, wide-plank floors, and hefty overhead beams present a sense of history in this spacious kitchen. A multi-level island helps make the expanse of space more intimate, and creates various heights for assorted kitchen tasks, including the one of enjoying the room from the elevated perch of Windsor-type bar stools. *Courtesy of Barbara Herr Kitchens*

Resource Guide

The following manufacturers and designers contributed imagery and expertise to this book:

Barbara Herr Kitchens
141 West Market Street; Marietta, PA 17547
Ph: 717-426-2287, Fax: 717-426-3005
kitchens@supernet.com

Thomas Bartlett Interiors
2151 Main Street; Napa, CA 94559
Ph: 707-259-1234, Fax: 707-259-1242
www.thomasbartlettinteriors.com

Bis Bis Imports, Boston
4 Park Plaza; Boston, MA 02116
Ph: 617-350-7565, Fax: 617-482-2339
www.bisbis.com

Canyon Creek Cabinet Company
16726 Tye Street SE; Monroe, WA 98272
Ph: 206-674-0800, Fax: 206-674-0801
www.canyoncreek.com

Charlotte Comer Interiors, Inc.
5609 Vickery Boulevard; Dallas, TX 75206
Ph: 214-953-0855, Fax: 214-953-0317
www.charlottecomerinteriors.com
ccomertx@aol.com

Susan Cohen Associates, Inc.
2118 Wilshire Boulevard, Suite 962; Santa Monica, CA 90403
Ph: 310-828-4445, Fax: 310-453-6996
www.susancohenassociates.com

Kitchen Concepts & Roomscapes, Inc.
159 Washington Street; Norwell, MA 02061
Ph: 781-871-2400, Fax: 781-878-8109
www.roomscapesinc.com

Crystal Cabinet Works
1100 Crystal Drive; Princeton, MN 55371
www.crystalcabinets.com

Downsview Kitchens
2635 Rena Road; Mississauga, Ontario, Canada L4T 1G6
Ph: 905-677-9354, Fax: 905-677-5776
www.downsviewkitchens.com

Elmira Stove Works
232 Arthur Street; Elmira, Ontario, Canada N3B 2P2
Ph: 519-669-1281, Fax: 519-669-1774
www.elmirastoveworks.com

Elizabeth Shapiro Murphy Interior Design
303 Chestnut Road; Sewickley, PA 15143
Ph: 412-749-6984, Fax: 412-749-1184

Gehman Custom Remodeling
355 Main Street; Harleysville, PA 19438
Ph: 215-513-0300, Fax: 215-513-1280
www.gehmanremodeling.com

Glidden paints
1-800-454-3336
www.glidden.com

The Hardwood Council
Ph: 412-323-9320, Fax: 412-323-9334
www.hardwoodinfo.com

Hearthstone Homes
1630 East Highway 25/70; Dandridge, TN 37725
Ph: 800-247-4442, Fax: 865-397-9262
www.hearthstonehomes.com

Henry Johnstone & Co.
51 West Dayton Street, Suite 200; Pasadena CA 91105
Ph: 626-395-9575, Fax: 626-395-9528
www.henryjohnstoneco.com

Interior Decisions, MC
140 Columbia Turnpike; Florham Park, NJ 07932
Ph: 973-765-9013, Fax: 973-765-0514

Jon Jahr & Associates, Inc.
833 Dover Drive, Suite 16; Newport Beach, CA 92663
Ph: 949-646-6098, Fax: 949-646-6099

JAY Interiors, Inc.
10614 Pagewood Lane; Dallas, TX 75230
Ph: 214-691-0842, Fax: 214-691-3165

Keener Kitchen Manufacturing Co.
560 West Boundary Avenue; Red Lion, PA 17356
Ph: 717-244-4544, Fax: 717-244-4050
www.keenerkitchen.com

The Kitchen Guild
3739 Pickett Road; Fairfax, VA 22031
Ph: 703-323-1660, Fax: 703-323-7348
www.KitchenGuild.com

Kountry Kraft, Inc.
PO Box 570; Newmanstown, PA 17073
Ph: 610-589-4575, Fax: 800-401-0584
www.kountrykraft.com

KraftMaid Cabinetry
PO Box 1055; Middlefield, OH 44062
Ph: 1-800-571-1990, Fax: 1-440-632-9533
www.kraftmaid.com

K T Highland, Inc.
89 Highland Drive; Lancaster, PA 17602
Ph: 717-396-0025/717-396-7878, Fax: 717-396-7920
www.kthighland.com

Mannarino Designs Inc.
Holmdel, New Jersey
Ph: 732-741-1444, Fax: 732-741-7441
www.mannarinodesigns.com

Merillat
1000 N Water Street; Milwaukee, WI 53202
Ph: 414-225-9592, Fax: 414-289-0417
www.merillat.com

Montana Ave. Interiors
1502 Montana Avenue, Suite 202; Santa Monica, CA 90403
Ph: 310-260-1960, Fax: 310-260-0110
www.montanaaveinteriors.com

Mouser Custom Cabinetry
2112 North Highway 31W; Elizabethtown, KY 42701
Ph: 270-737-7477, Fax: 800-472-5889
www.mousercc.com

Nancy Van Natta Associates
14 Baywood Terrace; San Rafael, CA 94901
Ph: 415-456-3078, Fax: 415-456-3079
www.van-natta.com

National Kitchen & Bath Association
687 Willow Grove Street; Hackettstown, NJ 07840
Ph: 908-813-3792, Fax: 908-852-1695
www.nkba.org

Plain & Fancy Custom Cabinetry
Route 501 and Oak Street; Schaefferstown, PA 17088
Ph: 1-800-447-9006
www.plainfancycabinetry.com

Quality Custom Cabinetry
PO Box 189; New Holland, PA 17557-0189
Ph: 717-661-6900, Fax: 717-661-6901
www.qcc.com

Kathryn Scott Design Studio, Ltd.
126 Pierrepont Street; Brooklyn Heights, NY 11201
Ph: 718-935-0425, Fax: 718-522-1456
www.kathrynscott.com

Signature Custom Cabinetry, Inc.
434 Springville Road; Ephrata, PA 17522
Ph: 717-738-4884, Fax: 717-738-6988
www.signaturecab.com

StarMark Cabinetry
600 E. 48th Street N; Sioux Falls, SD 57104
Ph: 800-594-9444, Fax: 800-550-2934
www.starmarkcabinetry.com

Stone Forest
Ph: 888-682-2987, Fax: 505-982-2712
www.stoneforest.com

Thermador
5551 McFadden Ave.; Huntington Beach, CA 92649
Ph: 1-800-656-9226
www.thermador.com

Timberpeg® The Artisans of Post & Beam
1-800-636-2424
www.timberpeg.com

Ulrich, Inc.
100 Chestnut Street; Ridgewood, NJ 07540
Ph: 201-445-1260, Fax: 201-445-1888
www.ulrichkitchens.com

Village
79 Madison Avenue; New York, NY 10016
Ph: 1-800-423-5881
www.villagehome.com

Waverly
79 Madison Avenue; New York, NY 10016
Ph: 1-800-552-9255
www.waverly.com

Wellborn Cabinet, Inc.
PO Box 1210; Ashland, AL 36251
Ph: 800-336-8040, Fax: 256-354-1874
www.wellborn.com

Wood-Mode Incorporated
One Second Street; Kreamer, PA 17833
Ph: 570-374-2711, Fax: 570-372-1422
www.wood-mode.com

Zook Custom Kitchens
100 Pleasant Run Road; Flemington, NJ 08822
Ph: 908-284-0658, Fax: 908-284-0758